David Bloom is director of the nationally recognized **Bloom School of Jazz** in Chicago, which he founded in 1975. Mr. Bloom taught at Northwestern University and Roosevelt University and instructed the United States Air Force Reserve Band.

A noted lecturer and writer, he is the author of instructional books including *Major Blues for Guitar; Minor Blues for Guitar; The II V I Book; Melodic Chords for Guitar; The Question and Answer Book; Melodic Linkage, Rhythms Around the Body;* and *Ear Training Sight Singing*.

At seminars, Mr. Bloom has lectured to student groups, including the American Institute of Graphic Artists, on the synergy and cooperation found in jazz groups. His book reviews and articles have appeared in the *Chicago Tribune* and numerous music publications.

Mr. Bloom began studying guitar at age nine. He later studied with blues-guitar icon Buddy Guy, noted jazz guitarist Reggie Boyd, and flute luminaries Joe Kainz and Chris Hinze before attending the renowned Berklee School of Music. From 1971 to 1980 he led his own band, for which he composed, arranged and played guitar and flute. A composer and arranger, Mr. Bloom has collaborated with noted Chicago conductor and arranger Cliff Colnot on "Duende," a critically acclaimed CD of original band jazz.

The Bloom School of Jazz

The mission of the Bloom School of Jazz is to perpetuate and promote the legacy of extreme individuality, unbridled imagination and deep feeling left us by the jazz masters.

The Bloom School of Jazz was established in 1975 by David Bloom. His original and innovative teaching methodology transcends a traditional approach to music, elevating music teaching to a study of universal human language. His teaching concepts have helped thousands of students - from beginners to professional musicians - make compelling and individualistic musical statements. The goal of the Bloom School is to seek and promote the development of each student's unique expression.

Acknowledgments

I would like to thank my mother for unending support and encouragement, Peter Lerner for his contributions to the book, Pat Fleming, Stu Greenspan and Steve Ramsdell for their helpful critiques, Reynaldo Certain for final layout, photography and graphic design, Tom Stern for copy editing and Lee Metcalf for music editing.

Minor Blues for Guitar Vol. I

By David Bloom

Table of Contents

Fire and Form Series

Fire and Form symbolize the two basic materials in any art form. Fire represents personal expression. Form is the structural design in any artistic statement.

Great art is an expression of individuality. Creative freedom, not mere imitative slavery, requires each person to find his/her own voice. Creating one's personal statement is the ultimate artistic endeavor. In order to make this unique statement, one must first master their craft. A serious artist must have both something to say and the means with which to say it.

Any musician who wills it can become a competent jazz player. The jazz artist must understand and be able to control the material which will form the design for his/her personal statement of emotions. Jazz improvisation is the celebration of the moment through the spontaneous musical expression of the gamut of human emotions. However, it is not sufficient for a jazz musician to only express emotion without direction. In composition or improvisation, it is not enough just to create musical ideas; they must be developed and go somewhere.

This series is designed to show the artist how to go anywhere in a specific way. With this series we transcend the limitations of idiom and style, to give the artist creative freedom using the universe of musical possibilities available in Western harmony. The basic material for all Western music is the same (the chromatic scale). Style is the artist's choice.

The **Fire and Form Series** does not deal with the presentation of different styles. It deals with musical relationships and possibilities. The style and specific use of the material is the prerogative of the player.

In this series, hearing the material has equal importance with playing the music. All music is sound. It must be heard, either as an active listener or as an active creator. The active musical creator must be able to hear a sound, either from an outside source or in his/her head, and then be able to sing, write, or play that sound. Music that is played or written without being heard first is merely chance music, in which the player does not have control of his statement. Instead of the desired vivid articulate and expressive musical statement, the player is only producing sounds.

Each book in this series can be learned in three to four months, giving serious students a new vocabulary and direction in their quest for self-expression through music.

Introduction

The heart and soul of great jazz is the blues. All jazz masters have developed their musical ear for playing jazz by first learning to play the blues.

When most guitarists learn chords, it's usually to play a song. They will sing the melody and play the same chords (position and fingering) every time. For them, being correct and functional is often more important than playing a fresher chord choice. One of the goals great jazz guitarists have is to vary their interpretation of tunes, playing the same chord types a different way every time they're played. Similarly, many advanced blues, pop, rock, or folk musicians have made the music sound fresh and unique by increasing their chord vocabulary.

Minor Blues for Guitar Vol. I is the first in a series of studies written to give the serious musician a melodic approach to playing chords. There are thousands of instructional books on the market today, each with its own compendium of chords and their positions on the guitar fretboard. Regrettably, these materials do not show students how to put chords together melodically to make great-sounding music.

Minor Blues for Guitar Vol. I solves this problem in a practical manner. To simplify the process, it takes only one 12-bar C-minor blues chord progression and creates 21 different melodic lines from it. The progression is basically a bebop minor blues. The only difference is the VI chord in the bebop minor blues is usually a dominant chord. I have chosen to use a VI major-type chord because it is fresher choice.

In order to link the chords effectively, we will be using **melodic chords**. All chords become **melodic chords** when played in succession because the notes at the top of the chords create a melody. For our purposes, I'll define a **melodic chord** as any chord that is chosen for both the chord type (Ma7, Dom7, etc.) and the note that is the highest pitched voice.

Each page of this straightforward and easy-to-use course becomes a powerhouse exercise for mastering the minor blues.

The course is divided into three sections:
1. Ascending Melodic Lines
2. Common Tone Melodic Lines
3. Descending Melodic Lines

The exercises in the first section make use of an ascending melodic line built on all the available chord tones and extensions of a Cmi7 chord (root, 9th, 3rd, 11th, 5th, 6th, and 7th). Here, each succeeding note in the top voice ascends by a major second (whole step) or a minor second (half step).

In the second section, the exercises employ a common letter name throughout the entire chord progression. Each of the chord tones and extensions available on the Cmi7 chord (root, 9th, 3rd, 11th, 5th, 6th, and 7th) are harmonized by each chord in the progression. To make this clear, each minor blues chord progression uses only one letter name for the entire page. The only time the melody note must necessarily change is when it is not a chord tone of the next chord. For example, the note D on C minor moving to Bb minor must change to Db to fit the new chord.

All of the exercises in the third section of this course use descending melodic lines from each chord tone available on the Cmi7 chord. Here, each note in the melody descends by a major or minor second. Overall, combining the seven tones of the Cmi7 chord in the three directions of the melodic lines yields a simplified yet effective means for mastering the technique of playing melodic minor blues chords.

By mastering each of the exercises in **Minor Blues for Guitar Vol. I**, serious music students will acquire greater fluency and melodic flexibility in playing chords. In a relatively short time students who work at this study will be moving chords around while comping and playing chord melodies or chord solos with the same melodic interest and variety of direction as they previously accomplished with only single-note playing.

ENHARMONIC NAMES
Many of the chords shown in this book have multiple names. The names given to chords are determined by the function of the chord within the progression. One name will make sense in one chord progression but will make no sense in another. The context is very important. For example, C#o7 in one progression will be named A7b9 in another, or Cmi6,depending on the context, can be called Ami7b5.

VOICE-LEADING
Very simply, the term "voice-leading" describes the way each note of a chord moves to the notes of the next chord. Smooth voice-leading dictates that the notes that are common between two chords remain the same while the others move to the closest chord tone of the next chord. For example, when moving from CMa7 (C-E-G-B) to F Ma7 (F-A-C-E) we notice that the notes C and E are common to both chords. To achieve smooth voice-leading the C and E will stay where they are and the B and G will move to A and F respectively. **Minor Blues for Guitar Vol. I** focuses on melodic movement and chord quality. In Volume II, bass movement, other melodic intervals and internal voice-leading will be covered.

COMPING
Many musicians don't think about melody when they are accompanying (comping) someone with chords. This becomes a tremendous oversight because when a chord progression is played, a melody will occur whether one is aware of it or not. The question then becomes, what kind of melody will it be - one with an interesting melodic shape that complements the soloist or one that lacks direction, and isn't responsive?

Practice Procedure

   I. You must know exactly what you're going to do BEFORE you start each exercise.

  II. Practice sessions must be goal oriented.

 III. Cleanliness in execution is imperative.

 IV. Gaining authority should be the goal of practice.

  V. Strict rhythm must always be maintained:
      a) Strict realization of rhythmic values
      b) Strict tempo maintenance

 VI. Use the entire dynamic range.

VII. Never practice longer than concentration can be maintained. To practice sloppily is not effective practice. It also shows a disrespect for one's abilities and potential.

VIII. Practice with a tape recorder to evaluate what you have achieved in each practice session. Listen back to the tape to hear how precise you were in your practicing. Did you achieve the QUALITY OF EXECUTION you were looking for?

 IX. You must learn to ENJOY YOUR PRACTICING. Take pride in the intensification and focus of your being. If it is a chore, proper relaxation and musicality will not happen.

  X. If you make or accept mistakes in execution, you are NOT practicing effectively.

How to Use This Book

There are many ways to use this book. The pace at which you cover this material is not important, but it is critical that you memorize one complete blues before proceeding to the next. Serious intermediate players will be able to competently learn all the material in this book in approximately three months. The criteria for excellence include being able to play each progression with clean execution, good time, and extreme dynamic contrast. As you progress, each new page will get a little easier, and after two or three pages are successfully memorized, things will move faster. As you start mastering each progression start to mix and combine the chords. In this way you will be able to play the same chord progression a myriad of ways, making it your own.

Procedure for development of the execution of chords.

1. Place all of the fingers specified by the diagrams. In this book I have given specific fingerings for chords, but you can fret the notes with whatever fingering is comfortable.

2. Play each string that's indicated individually to make sure each note is ringing with a clear tone, without buzzing or muting by another finger.

3. After you can individually play all the notes cleanly, play them all together, strum them, or pluck them.

4. After you can play all the notes in a chord simultaneously, try to play the next chord.
   Do the same procedure for each chord.

5. To develop strong chord execution each finger should move to the next note by the closest path. Keep fingers close to the fret board and slide up or down the neck to the next note if the same finger and string is used.

6. After you can cleanly play through this progression, you're ready to move to the next progression.

Minor blues comping exercises included in the CD

Track 1. Tuning note A 440.

Track 2. Play all chords long for their full duration.

Track 3. Play all chords short as 8th notes.

Track 4. Alternate between long and short attacks.

Track 5. Alternate between short and long attacks.

Track 6. Delay all attacks by an 8th note.
Play full duration.

Track 7. Delay all attacks by an 8th note and play short.

Track 8. Delay all attacks by an 8th note and alternate between long and short attacks.

Track 9. Anticipate all attacks by an 8th note and play full duration.

Track 10. Anticipate all attacks by an 8th note and play short.

Track 11. Anticipate all attacks by an 8th note and alternate between long and short.

Track 12. Play a rhythmic motif through the entire progression.

Track 13. Mix up the rhythms.

Track 14. Play less, laying out, not playing every chord.

Track 15. Freely using the chords in the book.

Track 16. Whisper, Talk, Scream dynamics.

Track 17. Alternate between very soft and very loud dynamics.

Track 18. Backgrounds for minor blues, slow tempo.

Track 19. Backgrounds for minor blues, medium tempo.

Track 20. Backgrounds for minor blues, up tempo.

Track 21. Backgrounds for minor blues, way up tempo.

Comping and Soloing Variations

Just knowing beautiful-sounding voicings and chord progressions is not enough. You must be able to play these chords with tremendous variety of attack, rhythm, and dynamics in order to make an expressive multidimensional musical statement. The following examples show you how to mix-up your attacks, rhythm, and dynamics.

Procedure:

1. Memorize the Ascending C progression on page 2.
2. Apply all examples (tracks) 2-17 of comping and solo variations to Ascending C.
3. Apply examples 2-17 to all the progressions in the book.
4. Freely mix all chords, rhythms, attacks, and dynamics using tracks 18, 19, 20, and 21.

Track 2. Play all chords long for their full duration. Use exact voicings from Ascending C.

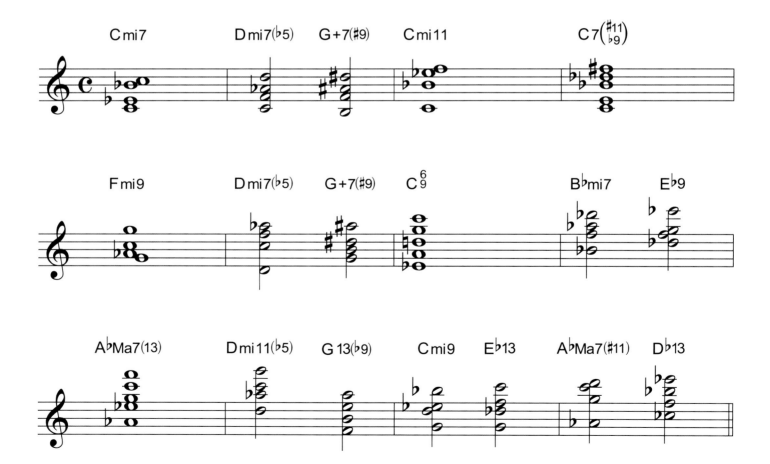

Track 3. Play all chords short as 8th notes.

Track 4. Alternate between long and short attacks.

Track 5. Alternate between short and long attacks.

Track 6. Delay all attacks by an 8th note. Play full duration.

Track 7. Delay all attacks by an 8th note and play short.

Track 8. Delay all attacks by an 8th note and alternate between long and short attacks.

Track 9. Anticipate all attacks by an 8th note and play full duration.

Track 10. Anticipate all attacks by an 8th note and play short.

Track 11. Anticipate all attacks by an 8th note and alternate between long and short.

Track 12. Play a rhythmic motif through the entire progression.

Track 13. Mix up rhythms. Listen and imitate.

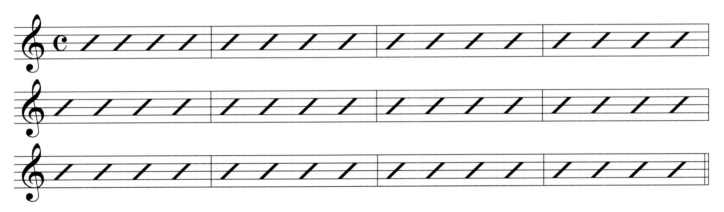

Track 14. Play less, laying out, not playing every chord. Listen and imitate.

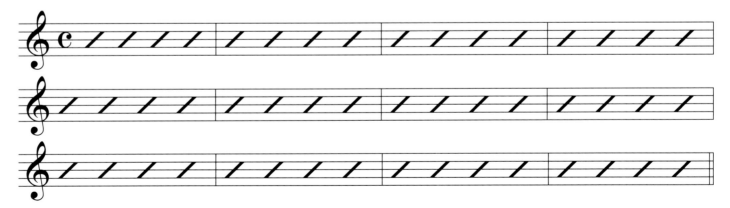

Track 15. Freely using the chords in the book with varied attacks and rhythm. Listen and imitate.

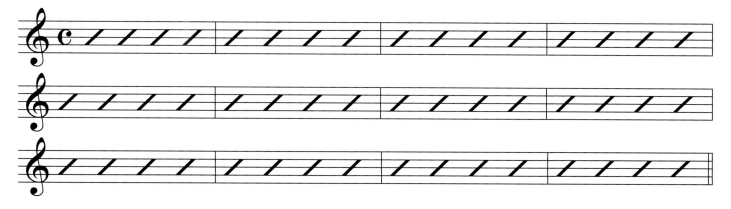

Track 16. Whisper, Talk, Scream dynamics.

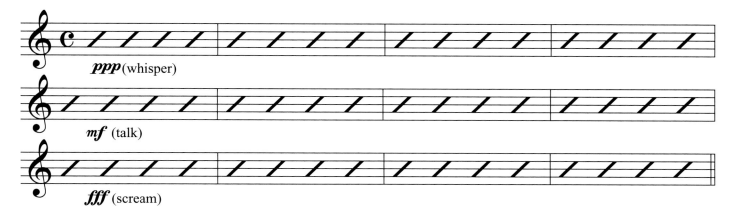

Track 17. Alternate between very soft and very loud dynamics.

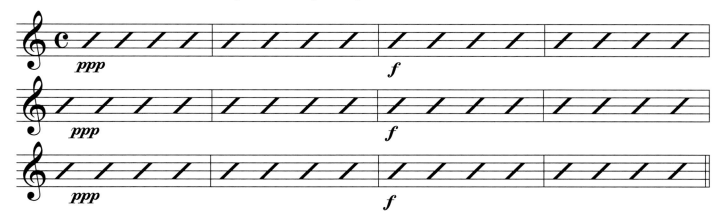

Dedicated to Wes Montgomery

SECTION I
ASCENDING BY SECONDS

In this section all of the melodic chord connections are by either minor seconds (half steps) or major seconds (whole steps). Seconds or scale-wise motion are the most common melodic movement in music. If you look at hundreds of standard tunes, you'll find that most of the intervals in the melodies are seconds. For example, "What Are You Doing the Rest of Your Life?" uses primarily seconds and only uses other intervals for relief or surprise.

Seconds are very easy to sing and easy to listen to. They gently and smoothly move us through time. Very often, seconds just move up and down sections of major or minor scales, creating a certain level of predictability.

Ascending melodies seem to take your ear up. As you listen to an ascending melody, you get a strong feeling that you are being pushed toward some kind of melodic resolution or climax. As pitches get higher, there is a building of intensity.

In the following chart, the first column names the chords in the minor blues progression on page 2. In the second column are the letter names of top notes of each chord. The third column shows the chord degree of each letter name in the melody.

Chord Name	Letter Name	Chord Tone
Cmi7	C	root
Dmi7(b5)	D	root
G+7(#9)	D#	#5
Cmi11	F	11th
C7(#11b9)	F#	#11
Fmi9	G	9th
Dmi7(b5)	Ab	b5
G+7(#11#9)	A#	#9
Cmi69	C	root
Bbmi7	Db	3rd
Eb9	Eb	root
AbMa7(13)	F	6th
Dmi11(b5)	G	11th
G13(b9)	Ab	b9
Cmi9	Bb	b7
Eb13	C	13th
AbMa7(#11)	D	#11
Db13	Eb	9th

Ascending C

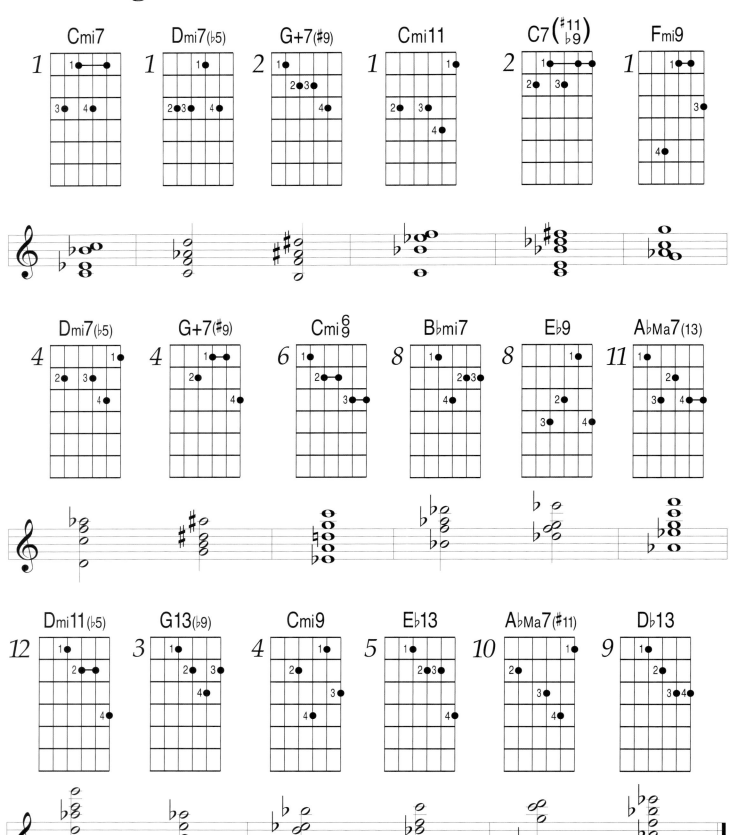

Ascending D

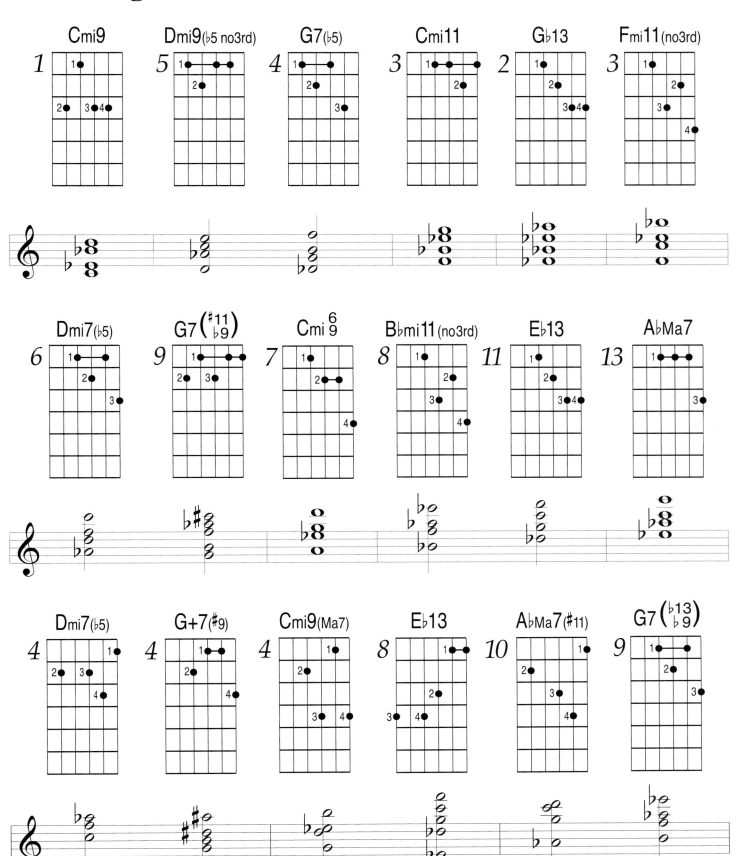

Ascending Eb

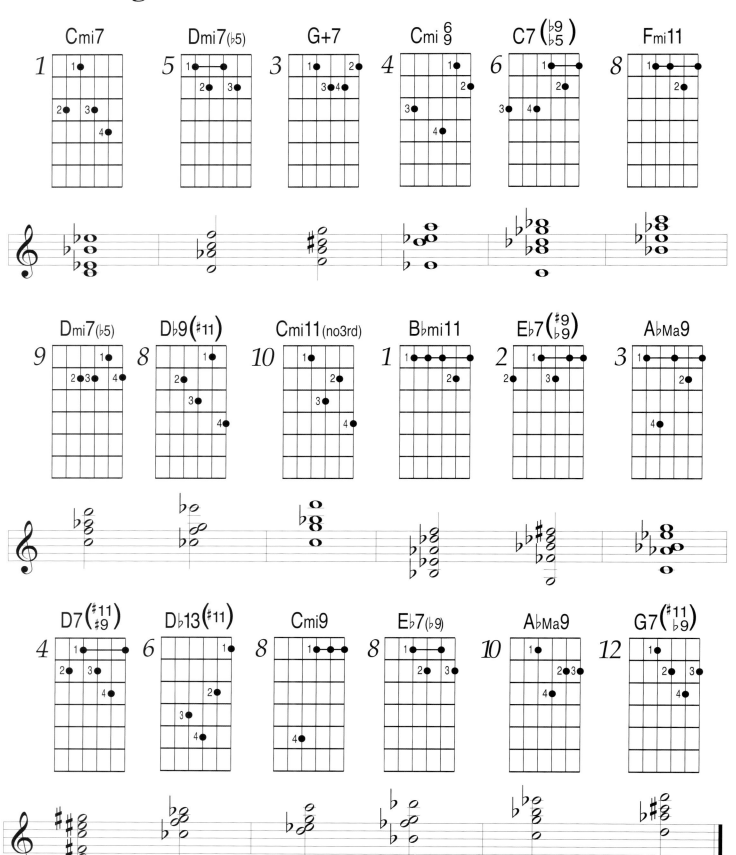

Ascending F

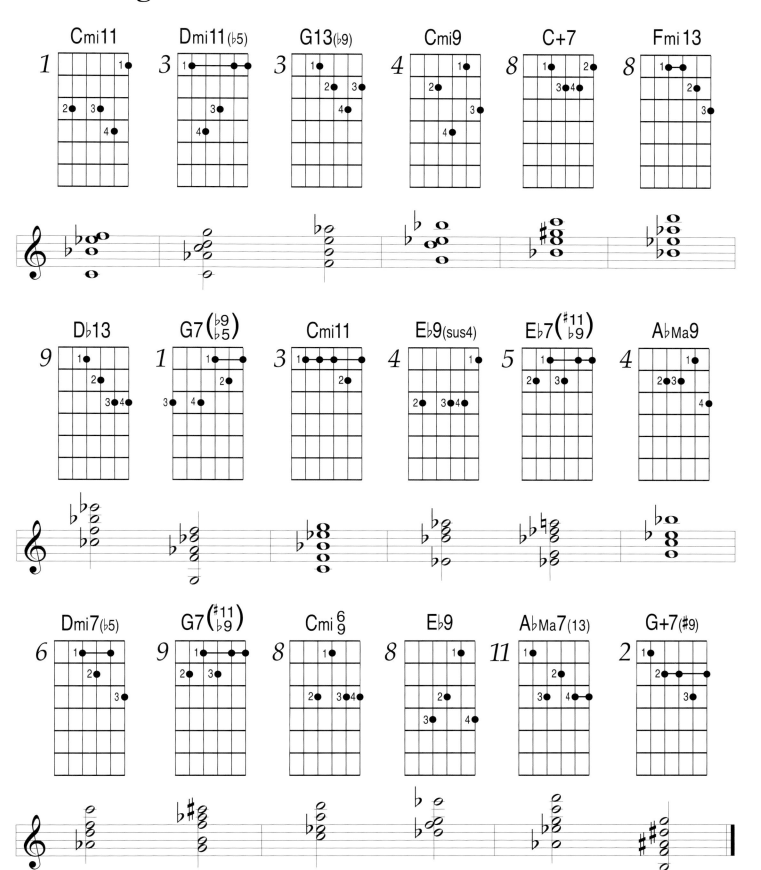

Ascending G

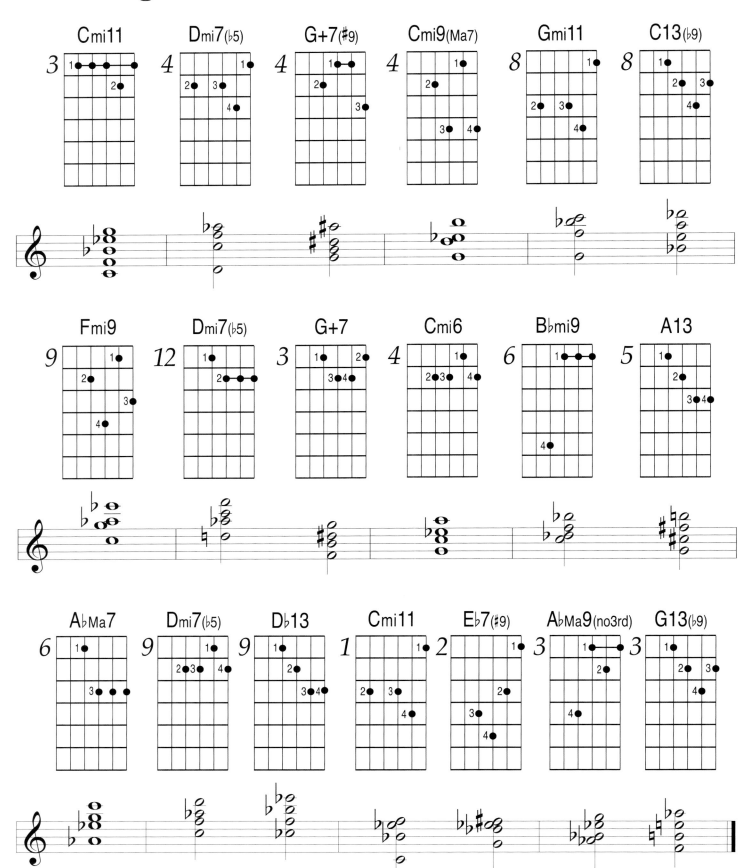

Ascending A

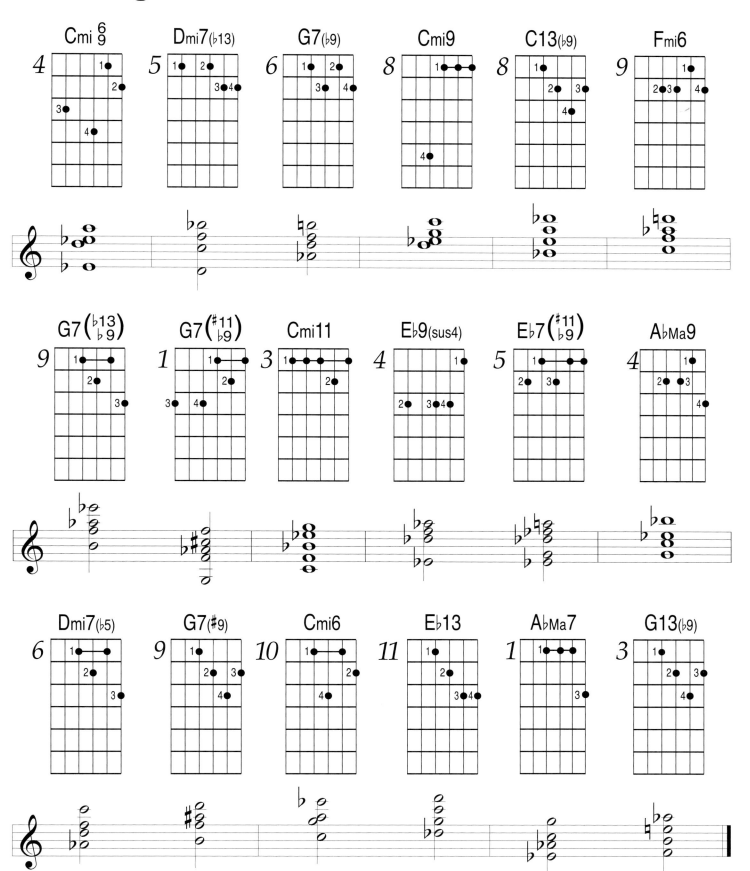

Ascending B♭

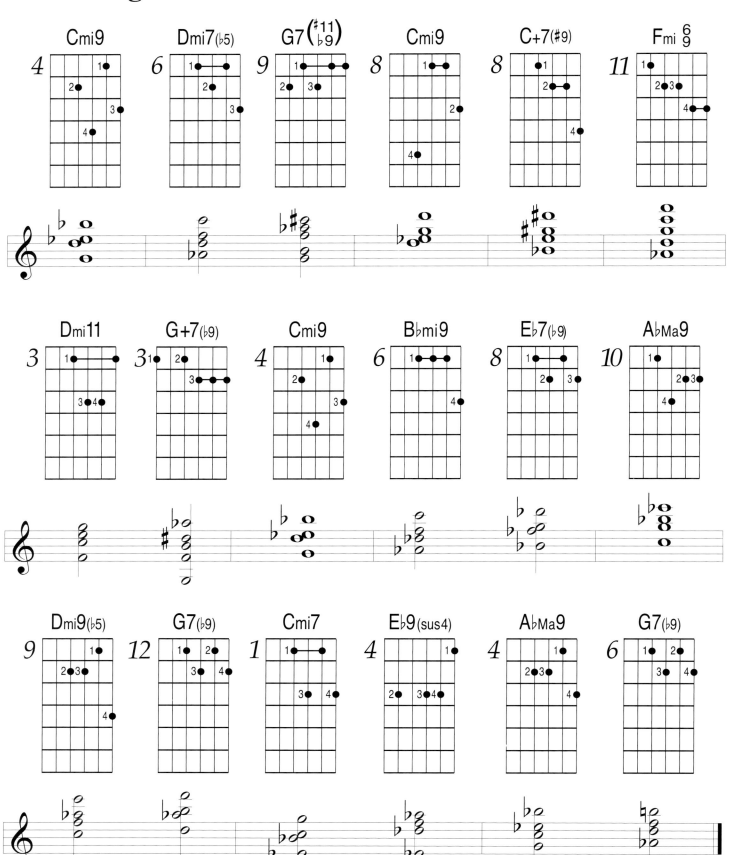

SECTION II
COMMON TONES

Common tones are a critical aspect of melodic chord linkage. They create continuity from one chord to another. When you sing common tones while the chord progression is played, the same notes actually sound different because each new chord recolors the notes. Also, using the same note on top of different chords connects the past, present and future. On each page in this section each letter of the musical alphabet ABCDEFG is in the melody for one entire page.

In the following chart, the first column names the chord in the minor blues progression on page 10. In the second column are the letter names of the top notes of each chord. The third column shows the chord degree of each letter name in the melody.

Chord Name	Letter Name	Chord Tone
Cmi9	C	root
Dmi7(b5)	C	7th
G9(sus4)	C	sus4
Cmi6	C	root
C+7	C	root
Fmi11	C	5th
Dmi7(b5)	C	7th
G9(sus4)	C	sus4
Cmi9	C	root
Bbmi9	C	9th
Eb(13b9)	C	13th
Abma7	C	3rd
Dmi7(b5)	C	7th
G9sus4	C	sus4
Cmi9	C	root
Eb13	C	13th
Abmaj	C	3rd
G9(sus4)	C	sus4

As you can see on page 10 and as shown in the chart, the C is used in the melody for the entire progression. In the first measure, C is the root of Cmi9; in the second measure, C is the 7th of Dmi7b5 and the sus4 of G9 (sus4); in the third measure, C is the root of Cmi6, and so on. On page 11 the note D is in the melody for the whole page. The only time it changes is when note D natural (meaning no sharps or flats) doesn't fit the chord. For example, when we get to Bbmi7, we have to flat the D or it won't fit the chord. This is true for all letters in this section. If the natural letter names don't fit the chord (meaning they aren't chord tones), they are sharped or flatted to fit. As you move through this section, you will see that some natural letters must change to fit the chord.

9

Common Tone C

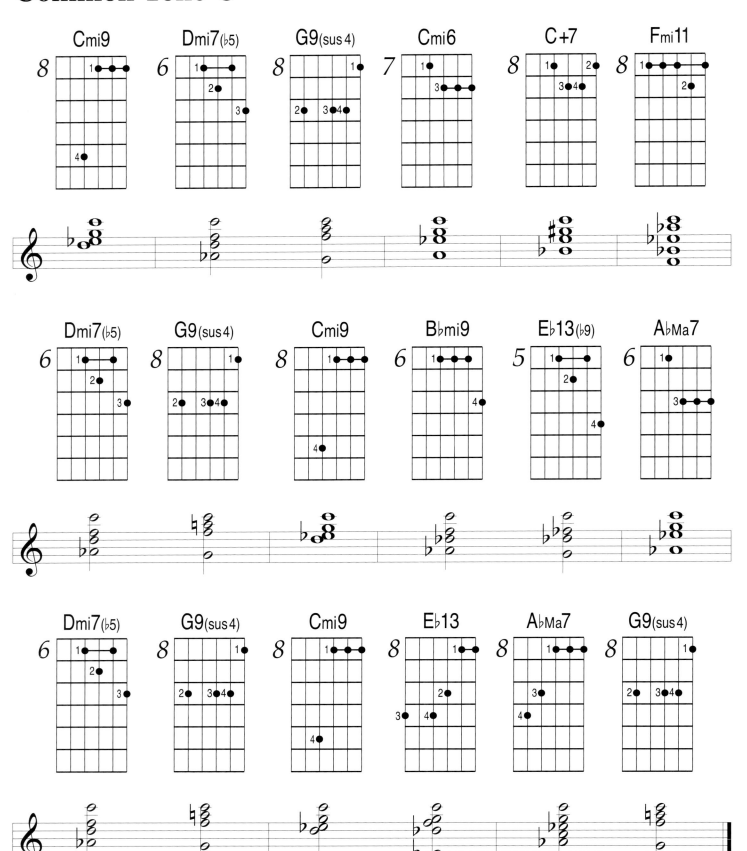

Common Tone D

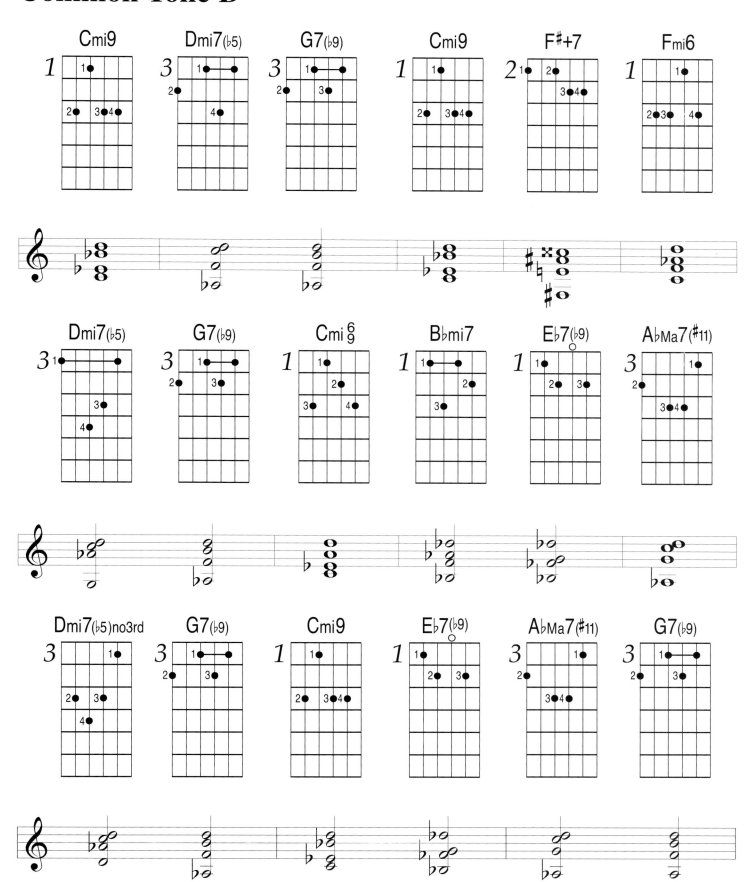

Common Tone Eb

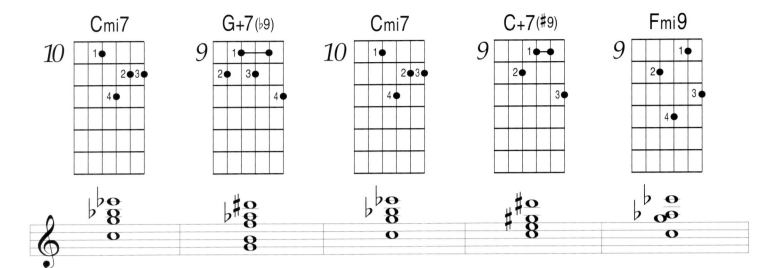

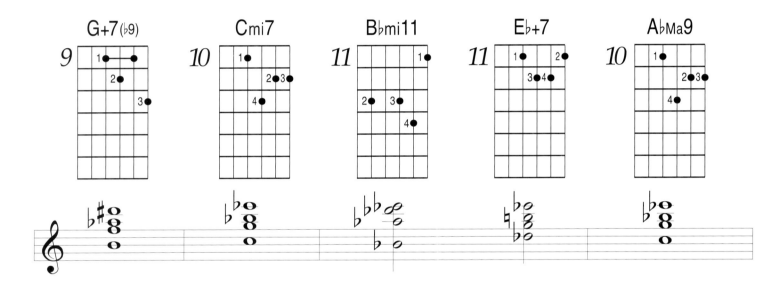

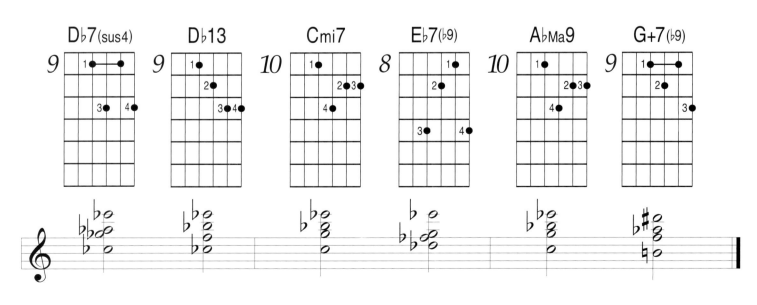

Common Tone F

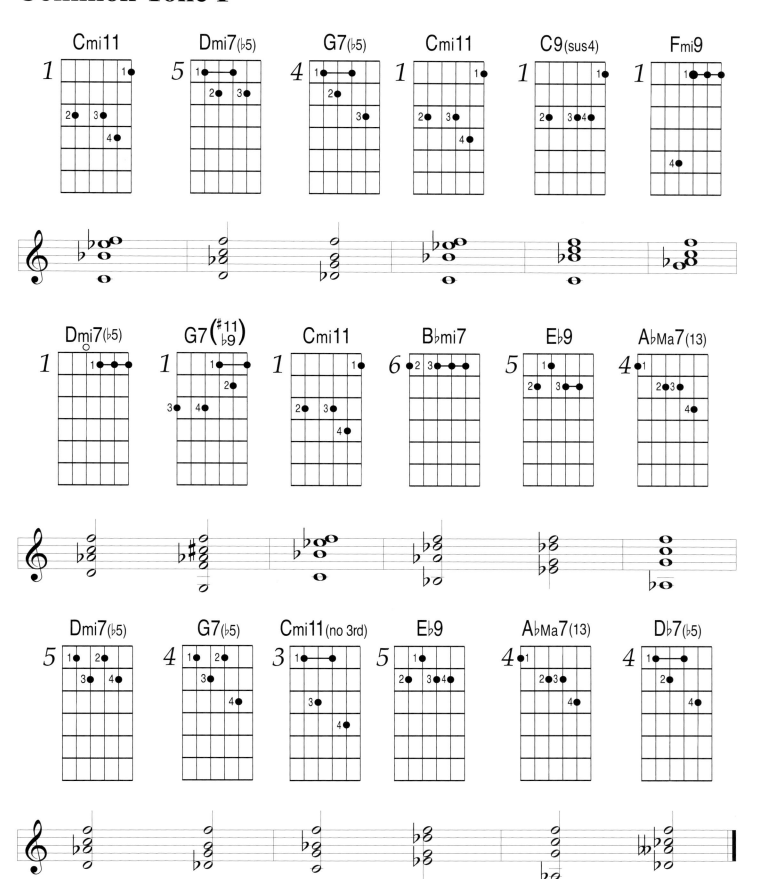

Common Tone G

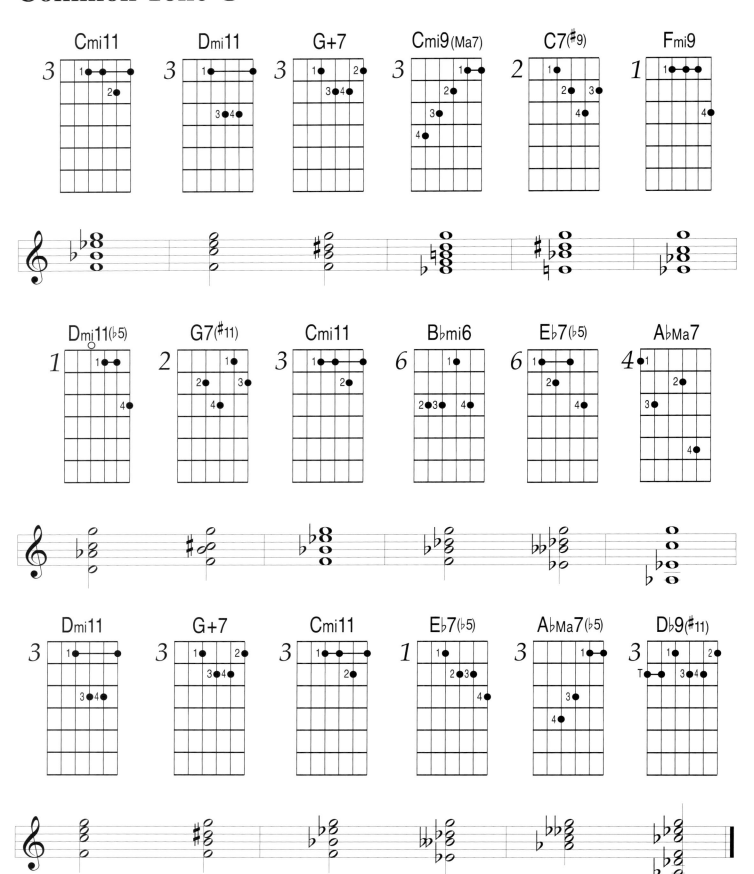

Common Tone A

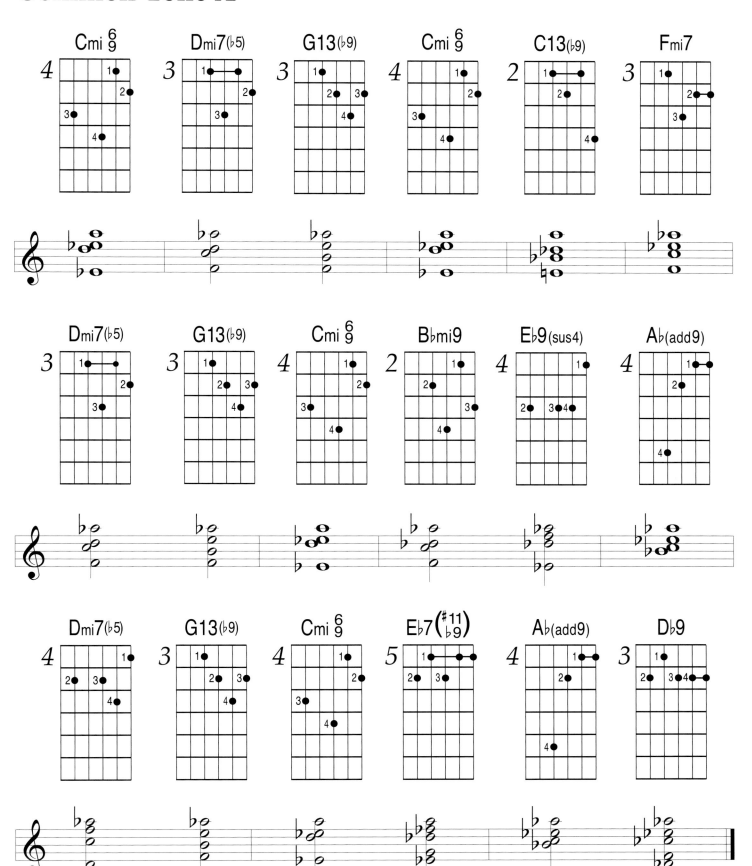

Common Tone B♭

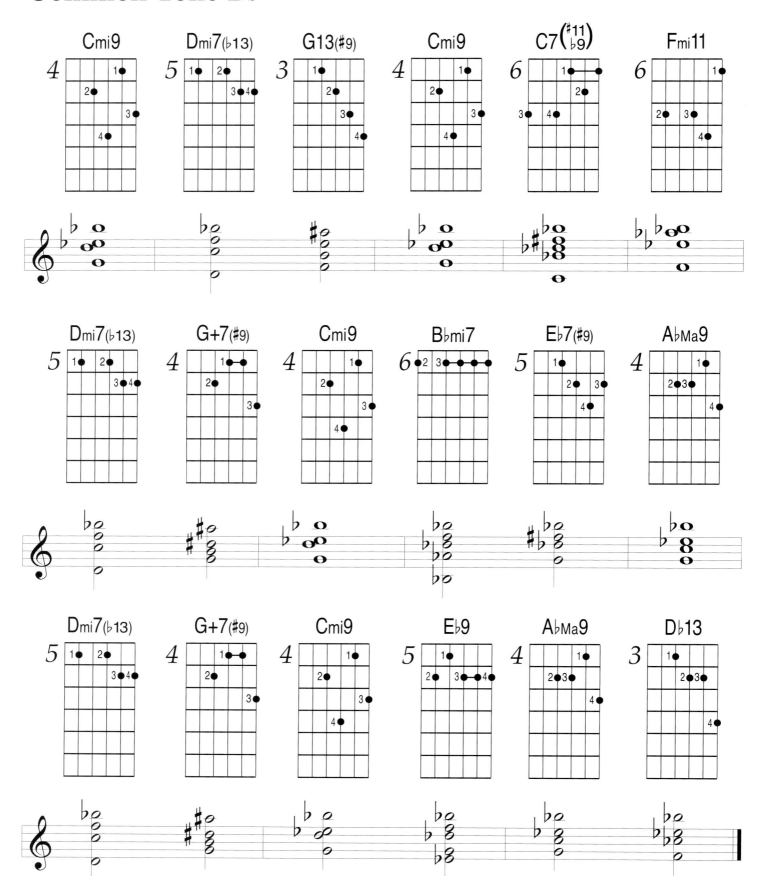

SECTION III
DESCENDING BY SECONDS

Descending seconds have much the same qualities as ascending seconds except the feeling is different when going down. The lower the pitches move, the subtler they become. Acoustically, it is easier to hear sounds in the middle and higher registers rather than in the lower register. This descending movement creates more of a subdued intensity and mystery than ascending seconds.

In the following chart the first column names the chord in the minor blues progression on page 18. In the second column are the letter names of the top notes of each chord. The third column shows the chord degree of each letter name in the melody.

Chord Name	Letter Name	Chord Tone
Cmi9	C	root
Dmi7(b5)	Bb	b13
G13(b9)	Ab	b9th
Cmi9(Ma7)	G	5th
C7(#11#9)	F#	#11
Fmi9	F	root
Dmi9	E	9th
G+7(#9)	D#	#5th
Cmi9(Ma7)	D	9th
Bbmi7	Db	b3rd
Eb13	C	13th
AbMa9	Bb	9th
Dmi7(b5)	Ab	b5th
G+7	G	root
Cmi11	F	11th
Bbmi11	Eb	11th
AbMa7(#11)	D	#11
G7(#11)	C#	#11

Descending C

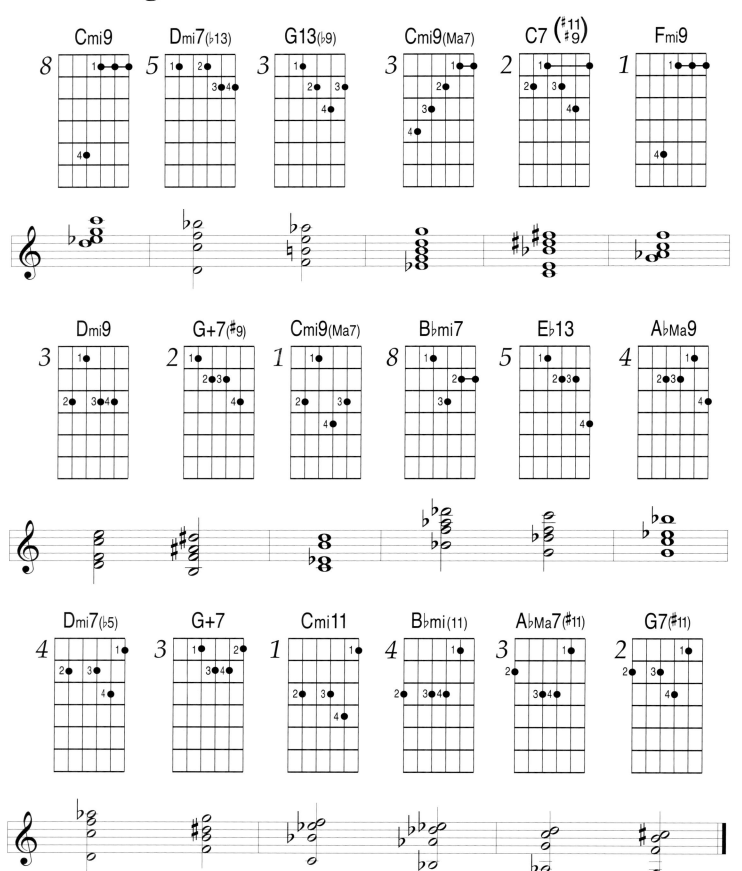

Descending D

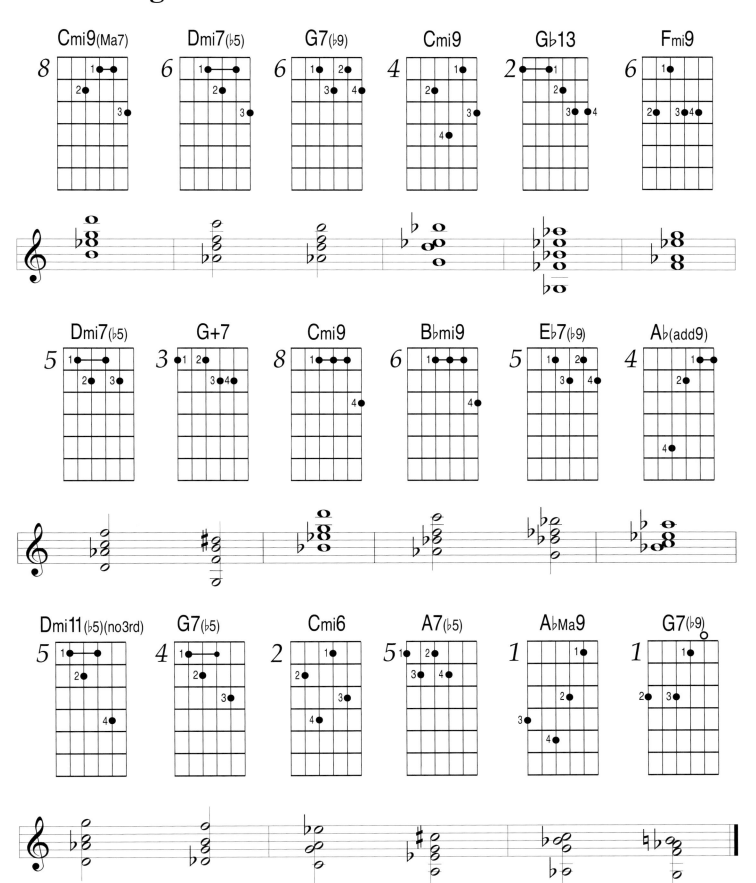

Descending E♭

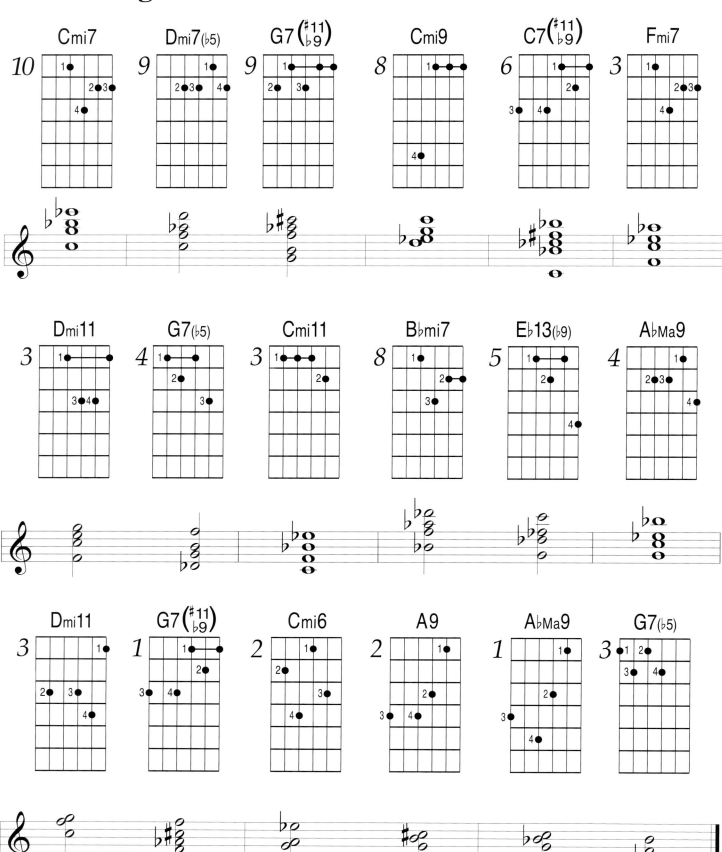

Descending F

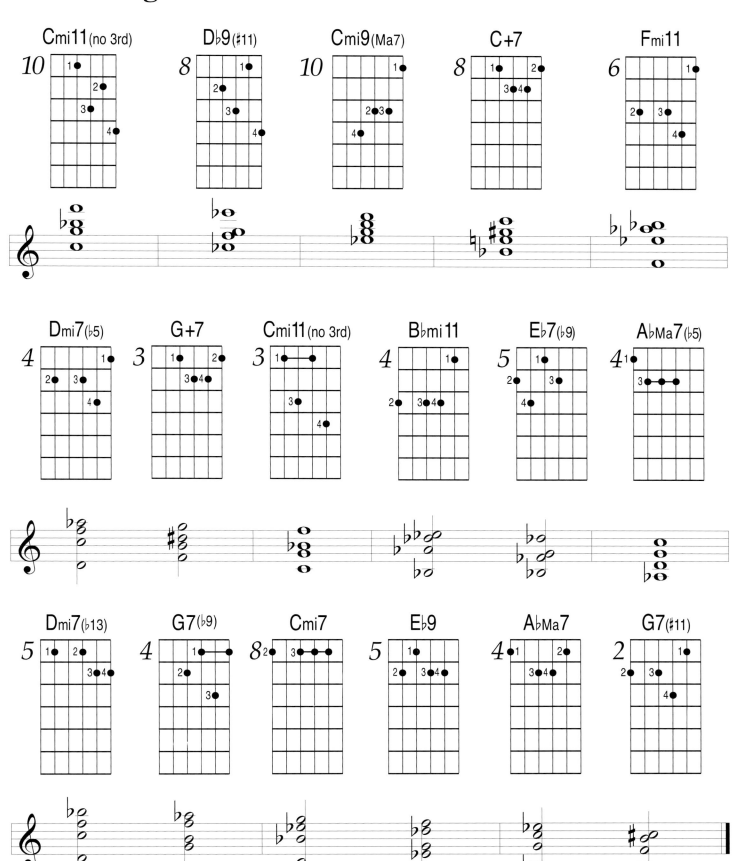

Descending G

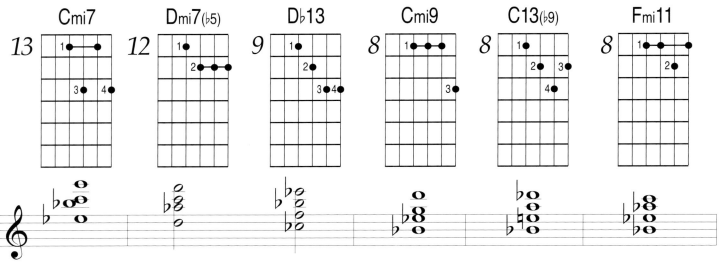

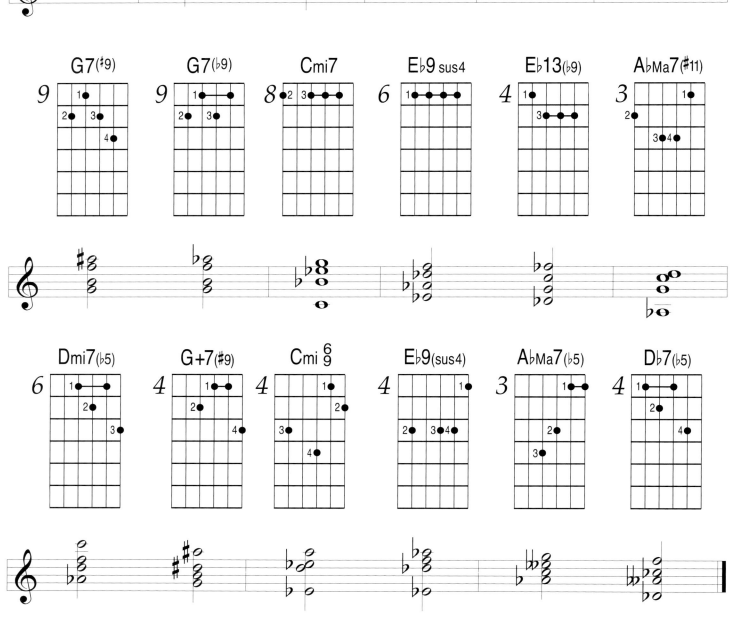

Descending A

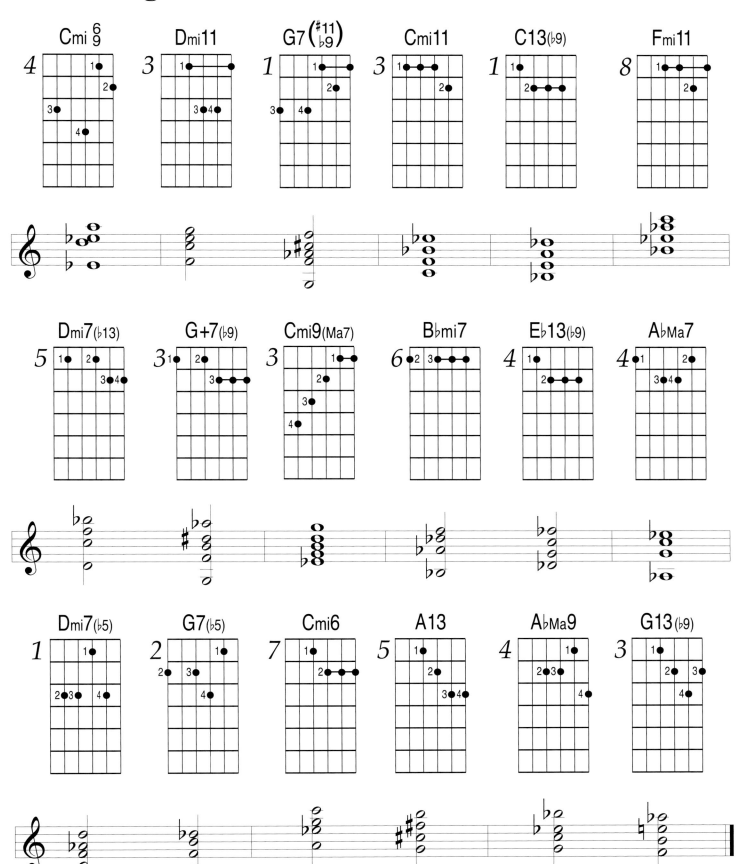

Descending B♭

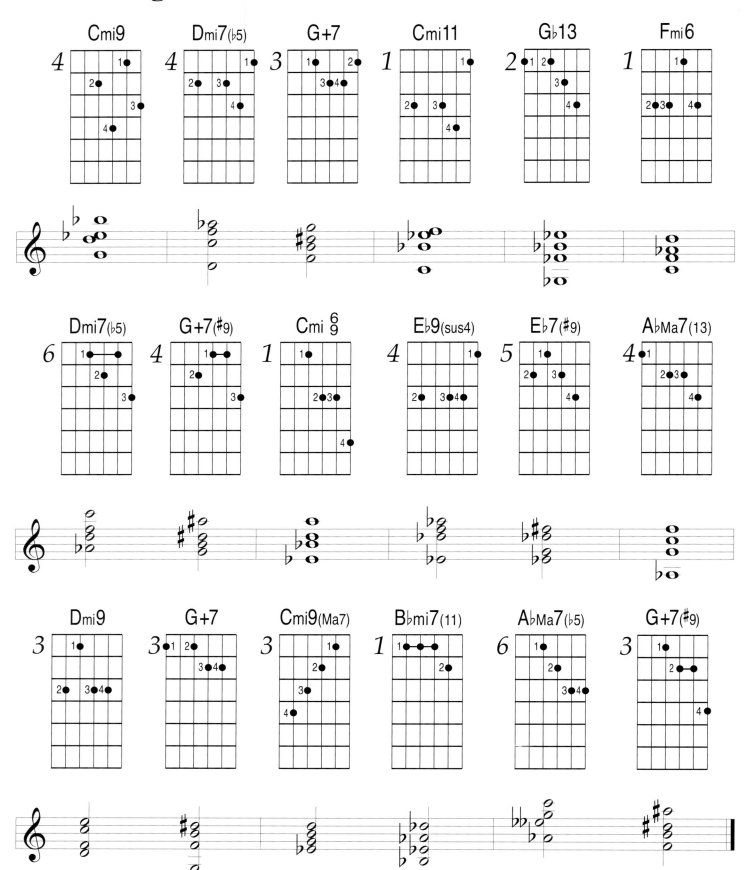

SECTION IV
EXERCISES

Now that you have learned the chord progressions in this book, it's time to check your recall and begin to combine the chords in your own way.

The first set of exercises will focus on memory. In the following exercises the first chord of each example is provided. On pages 26, 27, and 28, fill in the missing chords from the previously learned chord progressions. These exercises are used to check what you have absorbed and to reinforce what you have learned.

On page 29, create your own combinations of common tone, ascending, and descending chords. Sing the top notes of the chords as you play the progressions. This will help you to develop a melodic quality to your chord connections. With the chords that you have learned, you will be able to come up with as many variations of melodic minor blues chord progressions as you can imagine.

If every day you continue to search for new mixes of these chords, you will achieve fluency in the very near future. Serious and ambitious guitarists will regularly mix up and combine the chords in this book to create their own versions of minor blues. Remember that the goal is to make the minor blues your own.

Common tones

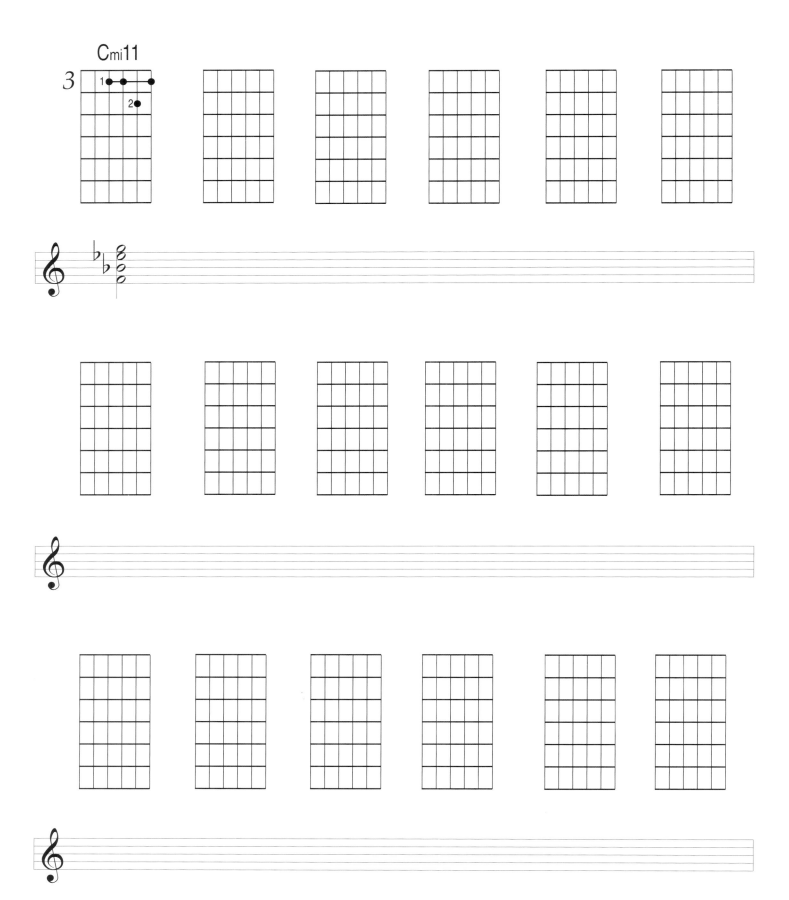

Asccending

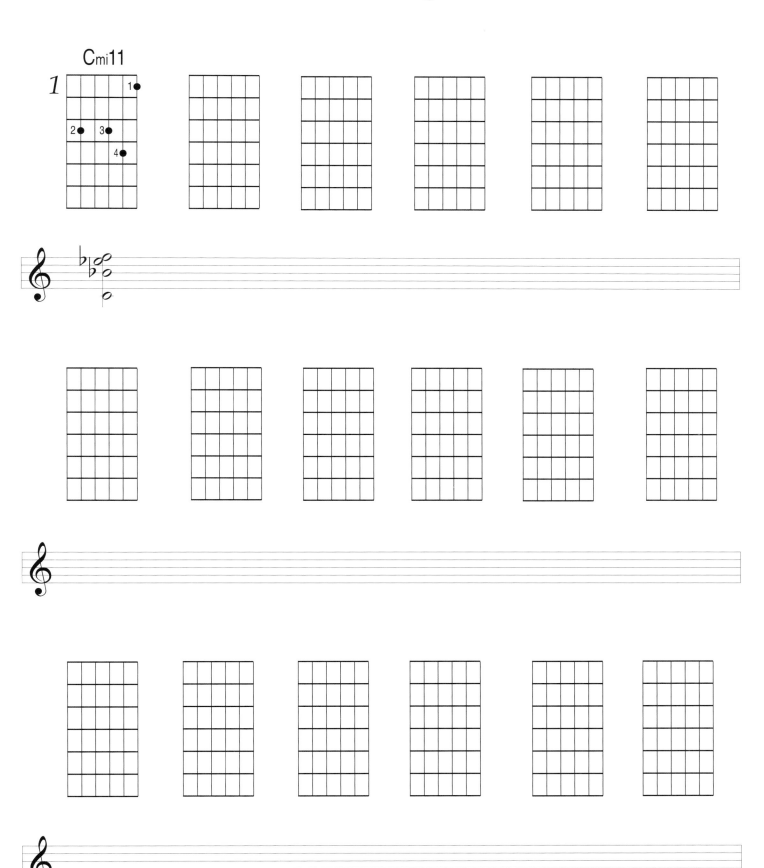

Descending

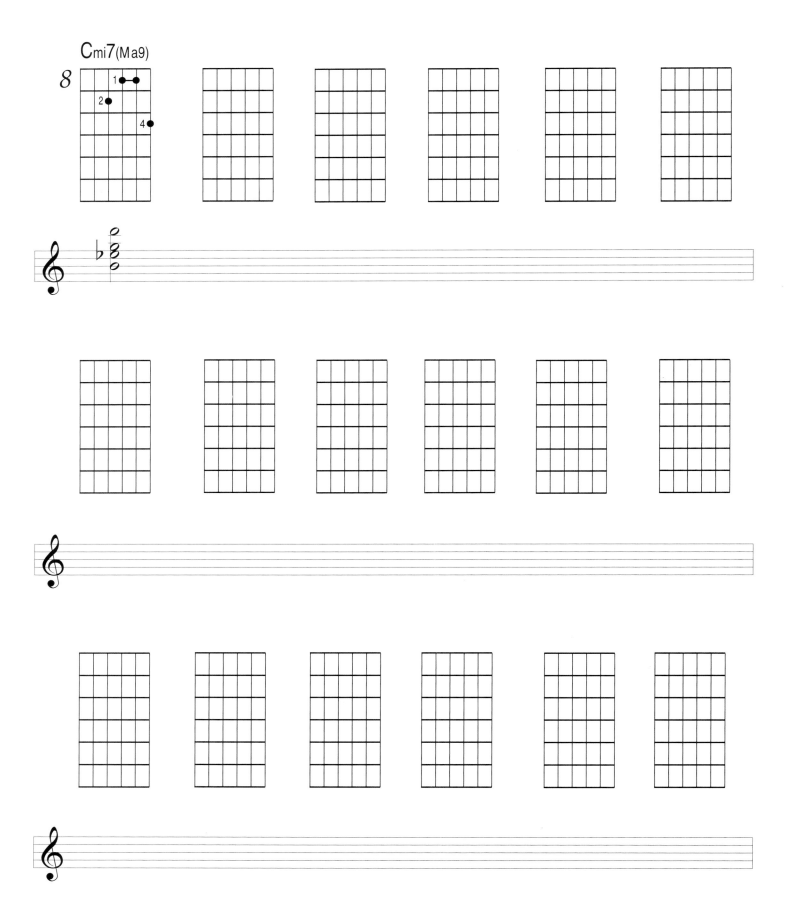

Mixing up common tones, descending and ascending

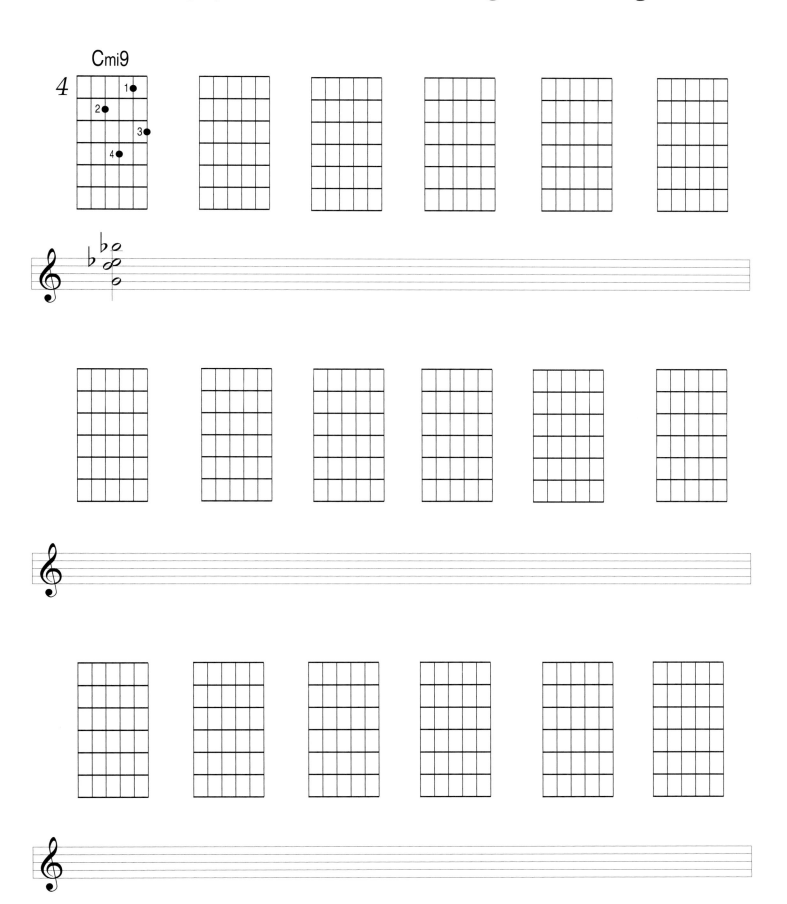

SECTION V
STORY TELLING

In the following minor blues progressions the chords are connected using intervals other than the common tones and ascending and descending seconds as previously covered. On pages 32-37, pay attention to the intervals used as well as the melodic ideas. Repetitive melodic motifs are used to create a kind of story line, and in each progression you can hear a motif or character that is introduced and then developed. Think of it as being like what happens to a character in a book or a movie. Just as his/her placement in a variety of situations illuminates the subtleties of his/her personality, so too will changing chords bring out the character of each motif. In the same way that you learn more about the character by seeing him in different situations, you will uncover new things about the motif as the chords proceed. The following progressions demonstrate this story-telling approach to chord playing.

In the minor blues "Now You're Hip" there are two main themes that tie the progression together. The first is the repetitive chord voicing starting with the second and third chords of the second measure and continuing throughout the progression until the turnaround. The second theme or motif is a combination of common tones and thirds. In measures one and two, the note F is a common tone for the first three chords: Cmi11, Dmi7(b5), and G7(b5b9). Then we have a third interval from F to Ab in G7(b5b9) to G13(b9). This two-bar melodic motif is repeated throughout the progression until the last two bars.

"Moving Up" and "Blooish Thirds" also use repetition to create interest and variety. You will want to note the melodic glue that binds each one together. As an exercise, try to make up a few short melodic motifs consisting of three or four notes that you can sequence through the entire progression, much like what you hear in the blues "Now You're Hip."

After you can play these progressions, apply the rhythms and dynamics from the Comping and Solo Variations on pages x-xv.

Now You're Hip

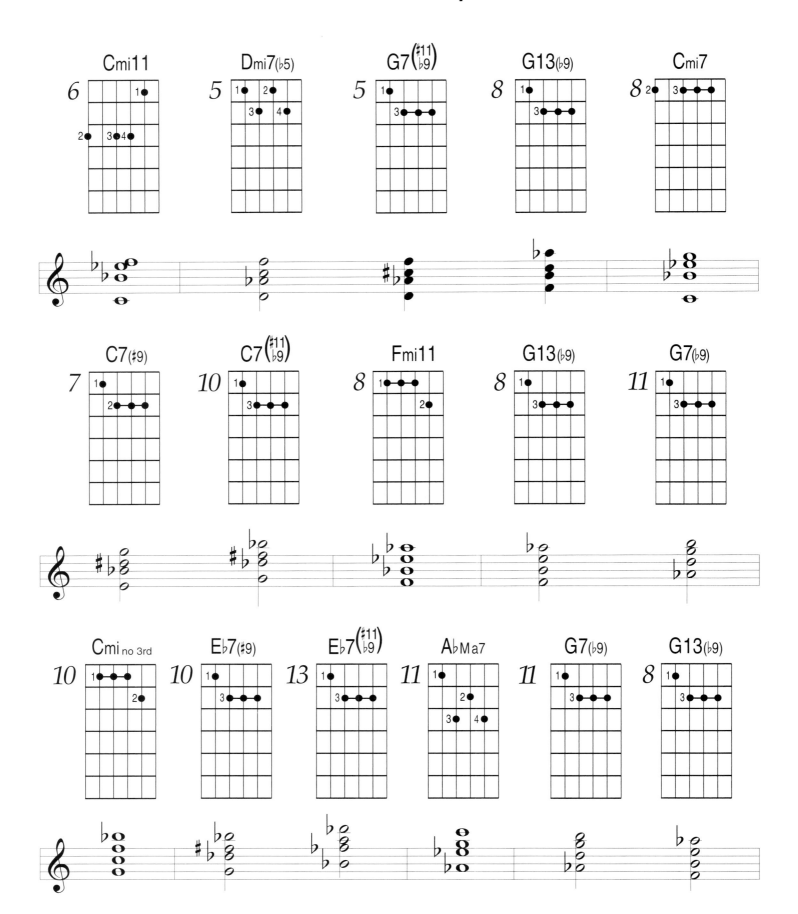

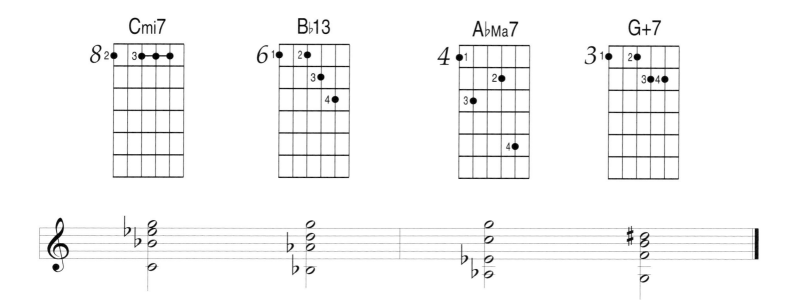

Moving Up

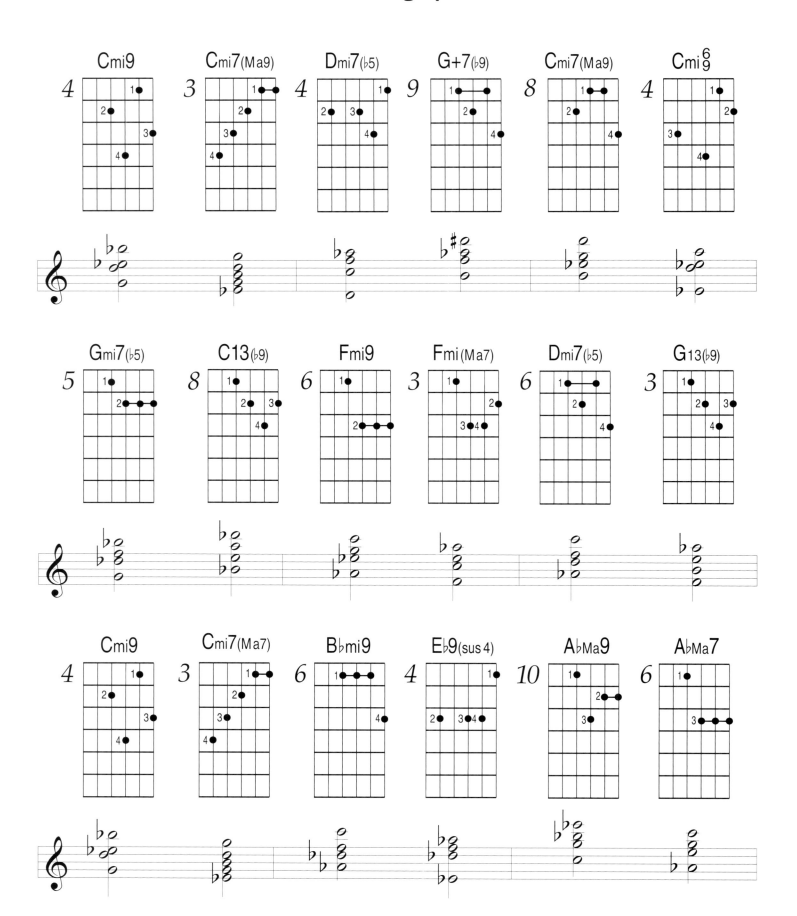

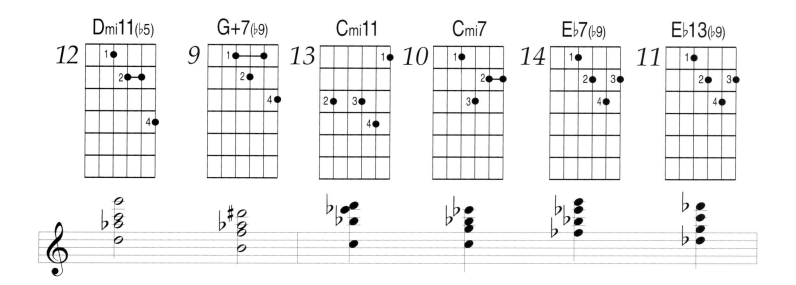

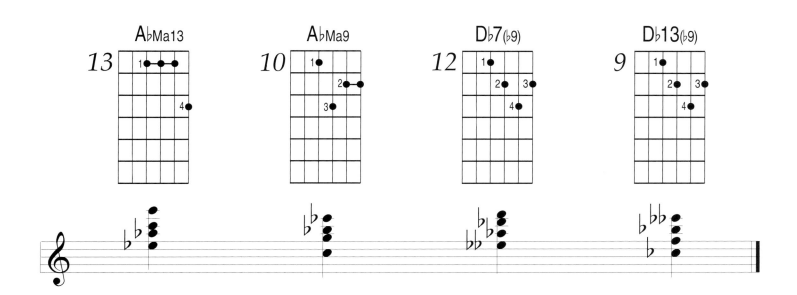

Blooish Thirds

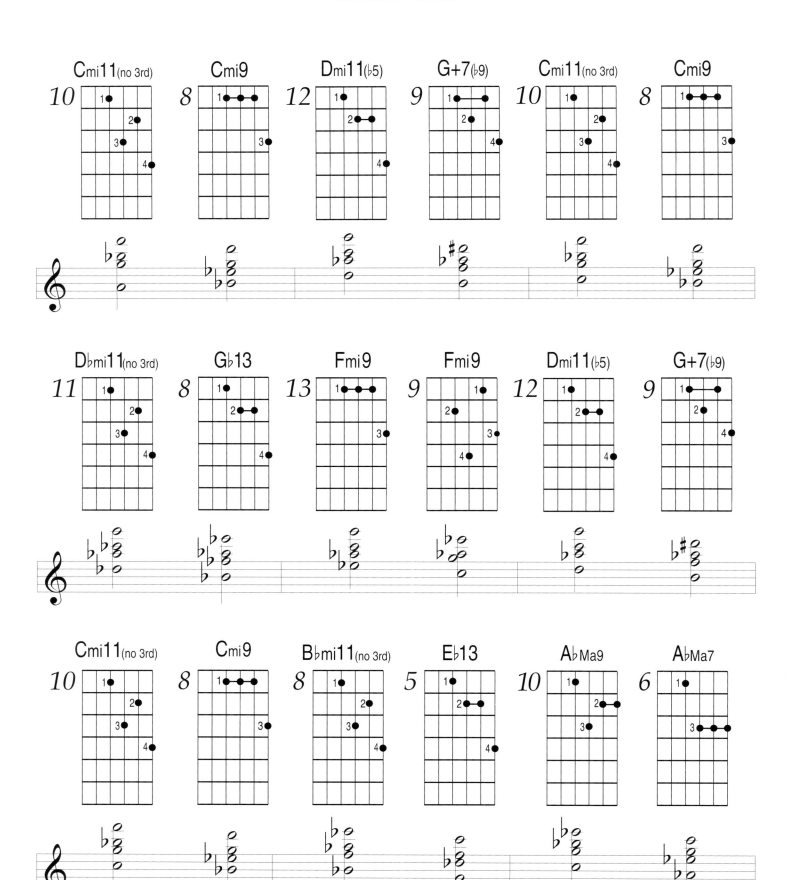

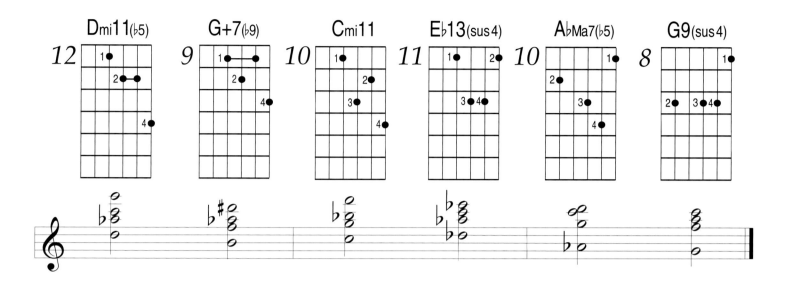

Congratulations! Now that you can play these progressions in C, transpose them to all keys.

I wish you good luck with your new chords, and may all your chord playing be melodic.

David Bloom

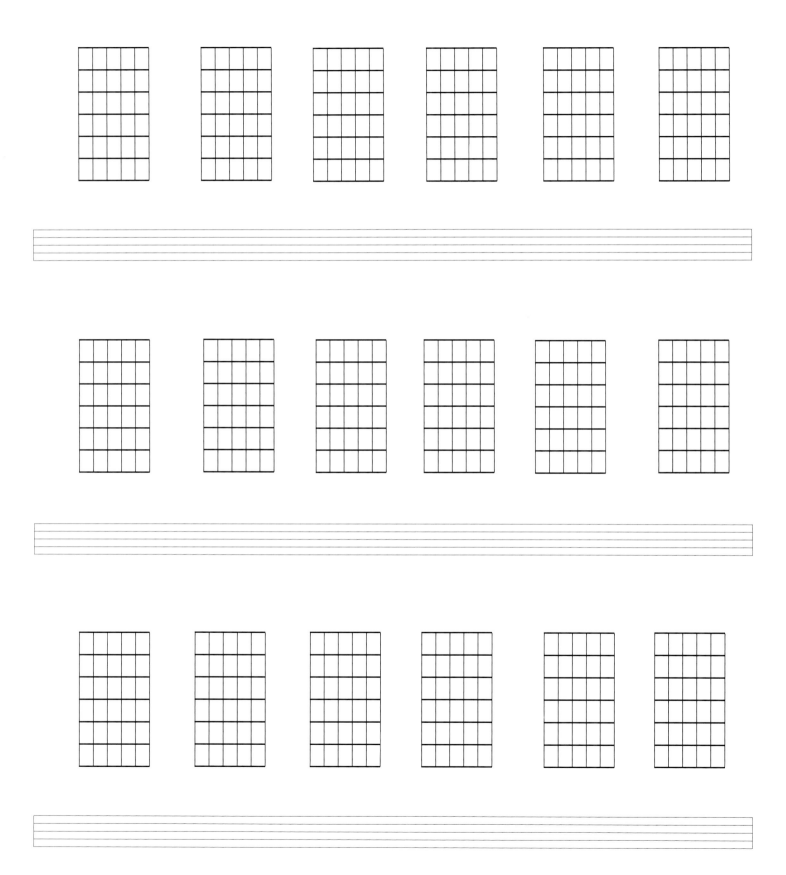

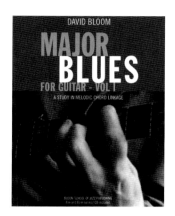
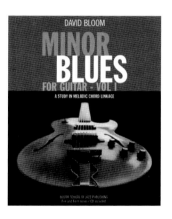
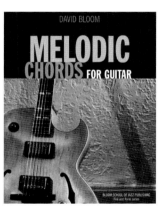

BLOOM SCHOOL OF JAZZ
218 S. Wabash, #600
Chicago, IL 60604
Phone: 312-957-9300
Fax: 312-957-0133

email: dbloom1@interaccess.com
www.bloomschoolofjazz.com